THE THREE THINGS

DIVORCED
CATHOLICS

NEED TO KNOW

BY MARY LOU ROSIEN

**Our
Sunday
Visitor**

www.osv.com
Our Sunday Visitor Publishing Division
Our Sunday Visitor, Inc.
Huntington, Indiana 46750

Nihil Obstat
Msgr. Michael Heintz, Ph.D.
Censor Librorum

Imprimatur
✠ Kevin C. Rhoades
Bishop of Fort Wayne-South Bend
January 30, 2017

Scripture quotations are from the *Revised Standard Version of the Bible — Second Catholic Edition* (Ignatius Edition), copyright © 1965, 1966, 2006 National Council of the Churches of Christ in the United States of America. Used by permission. All rights reserved.

Excerpts from the English translation of the *Catechism of the Catholic Church* for use in the United States of America copyright © 1994, United States Catholic Conference, Inc. — Libreria Editrice Vaticana. Used with permission.

Our Sunday Visitor Publishing Division, Our Sunday Visitor, Inc., 200 Noll Plaza, Huntington, IN 46750; 1-800-348-2440

ISBN: 978-1-68192-134-1 (Inventory No. T1860)

eISBN: 978-1-68192-138-9

LCCN: 2017931300

Cover design: Lindsey Riesen
Cover art: Shutterstock
Interior design: Dianne Nelson

PRINTED IN THE UNITED STATES OF AMERICA

About the Author

Mary Lou Rosien is a Catholic author, national speaker, and catechist. She is an RCIA coordinator, and she and her husband, Igor, are on the Pre-Cana team at St. Leo's Church in Hilton, New York. They have seven children. Mary Lou has written dozens of articles for *Today's Catholic Teacher*, AmazingCatechists.com, OSV.com, Catholicmom.com, and others. This is her second book published with Our Sunday Visitor. Visit her website at www.catholicfamilybootcamp.com.

Contents

Introduction

On my third wedding anniversary, my husband came to me and said he needed "to think some things out." I remember being shocked at the seriousness of his expression and asked, "What if you can't figure anything out?" He replied, "Then I will come back and we will figure it out together." He kissed me, left the house, and disappeared for three days.

When he returned, he told me he wanted a divorce. I didn't see it coming. I was completely dismayed and, in a state of disbelief, begged him not to do this to us. He ended our marriage anyway.

As a Catholic, the end of my union seemed unthinkable to me. I felt sad, lonely, confused, and abandoned. I couldn't understand how a loving God could let this happen. One of the hardest parts of this break up was the emotional pain and isolation it caused me. I truly believed that it takes two people to make a marriage and, equally, two to break one. The reality that one person can end it all was very hard for me. I spent months going through all the stages of grief: denial, anger, bargaining, depression, and, finally, acceptance (following the Kübler-Ross model).

I wish I could give those of you suffering through a divorce a quick way to fast-forward through this pain, but it takes time. I remember becoming so depressed that I wanted to give up. If I am completely honest, I even considered the thought of ending my own life at one point, but I had survived the suicide of my younger brother a few years before and knew firsthand the pain and devastation it caused. I also knew, deep down, that pain is an emotion. Emotions are not accurate in predicting the outcome of situations. Emotions change, and that is the thought I clung to in my darkest moments. I held fast to the family members I loved and committed myself to living so I would not be the cause of any more pain.

When the depression lifted, I was able to see my life as it was, and I made the decision to live my life in joy. (Surviving this suffering was the inspiration for my book *The Joy-Filled Broken Heart*, CreateSpace, 2016.)

Over the next few years, I would come to terms with the Church's teachings on marriage, divorce, annulment, and remarriage. Eventually, I was trained as an annulment-case sponsor. This journey was difficult and, at times, frustrating.

In preparation for writing this book, I interviewed Catholics who have been through a divorce and discussed with them the many challenges presented through that process. I have discovered some common threads for those who found joy following a divorce. These commonalities center around handling — with the help of the Church — 1) Emotional hurt, 2) The annulment process, and 3) Separation from the sacraments. I hope to share those insights. My sincere desire is that in these pages you will find hope and a path to joy following your own divorce or for those in your life affected by divorce.

Prayer
*Lord, guide me to the insights I need
to help me find joy.*

Questions for Reflection

1. What do I hope to find in this booklet?

2. What am I struggling with the most following my divorce?

CHAPTER ONE

Understanding What the Church Teaches about Divorce

Trust the LORD with all your heart,
and do not rely on your own insight.
In all your ways acknowledge him,
and he will make straight your paths.
— Proverbs 3:5-6

"I broke a sacrament when I got divorced!" Those are the words of a faithful Catholic who thought she had let herself, her Church, and God down after her marriage fell apart. Many faithful suffer greatly not only due to the actual emotional pain of the ending of a marriage but also by complications due to misunderstandings of the Church's teachings on marriage and divorce. Additional anguish can be experienced by Catholics who were trying to live their lives as a sacrament and think they have disappointed God by failing.

To restore joy to these individuals, we must first look at what the Catholic Church actually teaches about marriage and divorce.

The first distinction that the Catholic Church makes where marriage is concerned is the difference between what is legal (according to civil law) and what is valid. If a couple complies with the rules of a certain state regarding marriage, their marriage is civilly legal. Should that marriage end and the correct paperwork be filed, that couple is legally divorced.

The Church considers the Sacrament of Matrimony a marriage between a man and a woman making a vow and conferring the sacrament on each other, with the witness of a priest or deacon along with two other witnesses. This is a higher call to a vocation of marriage rather than just a legal standing in the community. That is why the Church teaches the permanence of Christian marriage.

To enter into this sacrament of marriage, the couple must examine and agree to several Church teachings:

1. The individuals must be "free" to marry in the Church. There cannot be any coercion, pressure, or outstanding commitments (such as a previous marriage that has not been annulled) that would preclude the individuals from marrying.

2. The couple must understand the Church's teaching on the permanence of marriage.

3. Each individual must have clarity on what total faithfulness to the other entails. For example, there cannot be a connection to anyone or anything that would threaten that faithfulness (old girlfriend or boyfriend, pornography addiction, internet relationship, etc.).

4. The betrothed are expected to be open to life, have a desire to be "fruitful," and possess full knowledge of Catholic teachings on sexuality and procreation.

If any of these elements is not present or is disguised at the time of the marriage ceremony, the marriage may be annulled, declaring that the union did not exist. When a marriage is dissolved legally and one seeks a declaration of nullity, a Church tribunal can examine the union to see if a valid union really existed.

But does the Church ever say that a separation or ending of the marital union is acceptable? The *Catechism of the Catholic Church* (Section IV: Offenses against Marriage) addresses the subject of divorce in the following way:

> **2382** The Lord Jesus insisted on the original intention of the Creator who willed that marriage be indissoluble. He abrogates the accommodations that had slipped into the old Law.

Between the baptized, "a ratified and consummated marriage cannot be dissolved by any human power or for any reason other than death."

2383 The *separation* of spouses while maintaining the marriage bond can be legitimate in certain cases provided for by canon law.

If civil divorce remains the only possible way of ensuring certain legal rights, the care of the children, or the protection of inheritance, it can be tolerated and does not constitute a moral offense.

2384 *Divorce* is a grave offense against the natural law. It claims to break the contract, to which the spouses freely consented, to live with each other till death. Divorce does injury to the covenant of salvation, of which sacramental marriage is the sign. Contracting a new union, even if it is recognized by civil law, adds to the gravity of the rupture: the remarried spouse is then in a situation of public and permanent adultery:

> If a husband, separated from his wife, approaches another woman, he is an adulterer because he makes that woman commit

adultery; and the woman who
lives with him is an adulteress,
because she has drawn another's
husband to herself. (St. Basil,
Moralia 73,1)

2385 Divorce is immoral also because
it introduces disorder into the family
and into society. This disorder brings
grave harm to the deserted spouse, to
children traumatized by the separation
of their parents and often torn between
them, and because of its contagious effect
which makes it truly a plague on society.

2386 It can happen that one of the
spouses is the innocent victim of a divorce decreed by civil law; this spouse
therefore has not contravened the moral
law. There is a considerable difference
between a spouse who has sincerely tried
to be faithful to the sacrament of marriage and is unjustly abandoned, and one
who through his own grave fault destroys
a canonically valid marriage.

Elsewhere, concerning "Matrimonial Consent,"
the *Catechism* states:

1629 For this reason (or for other reasons that render the marriage null and

void) the Church, after an examination of the situation by the competent ecclesiastical tribunal, can declare the nullity of a marriage, i.e., that the marriage never existed. In this case the contracting parties are free to marry, provided the natural obligations of a previous union are discharged.

These teachings may seem difficult and even harsh, but Christ, through his Church, views marriage as something spouses are called to for life; therefore, the circumstances under which a marriage would be declared annulled must be serious and indisputable.

Annulments usually address the readiness and understanding of the man and woman prior to the wedding vows. If the marriage bond was not entered into freely, faithfully, fruitfully, and with the expectation of "until death do us part," it is possible that a valid marriage did not exist. Considering that many go into marriage at a young age, immaturity may play a part in the spouses' ability to fully comprehend the promises of the marriage union.

———

For one pain endured with joy,
we shall love the good God more.
— St. Thérèse of Lisieux

———

Special struggles for divorced Catholics

- Profound sense of disenfranchisement (disconnectedness)
- Exaggerated sense of failure, feeling they have let God down
- Guilt
- Overwhelmed at process of annulment
- Possible separation from the sacraments
- Pain during Scripture readings on marriage, love, or family
- Feeling judged
- Loneliness among others of the same faith
- Embarrassment
- Economic struggles

These challenges are very real to the person experiencing them, and special sensitivity is required when talking to divorced Catholics. It is wise to offer support in the struggle and recognize the added confusion during this painful time. I remember sitting in Mass seeking solace and comfort as I struggled with my separation from my husband. The reading that day was on the obligation of husbands to their wives (see Eph 5) and vice versa. I could not contain my grief. I felt that I was being reinjured by my own failures and my husband's rejection. We made those vows, so how could this be happening?

Divorce can also bring parenting challenges, as many discover. Pam* stated that no one gave her any practical advice on parenting alone or on helping her children navigate the teen years — even things like applying for colleges (for her children) were outside her field of knowledge. Finding herself alone and without any guidance made everything more difficult and frustrating for her. This led to increased loneliness and a feeling that she had failed, not only in marriage but in aspects of parenting as well.

Others experience huge changes in economic status and financial security following divorce. These issues cannot be ignored by a compassionate Church, and divorced Catholics can lead the way in bringing them into the conscience of their communities.

————

Priests have a duty to "accompany [the divorced and remarried] in helping them to understand their situation according to the teaching of the Church and the guidelines of the Bishop."
— Amoris Laetitia, *300.*

————

* All names have been changed to protect anonymity of those interviewed.

Prayer

My heart has been so broken by this experience, Lord. If I have had misunderstandings about Church teachings that have added to that heartbreak, please reveal them to me and heal me.

Questions for Reflection

1. Do I need to discuss my situation with a priest, deacon, or spiritual adviser to better understand what the Church teaches about marriage and divorce?

2. Have I been angry at the Church or God because of my divorce or misunderstanding about teachings on it?

3. How can I reconcile my situation with what the Church teaches?

CHAPTER TWO

Lead Us Not into Temptation

God has led you these forty years in the wilderness,
that he might humble you, testing you to know
what was in your heart, whether you would
keep his commandments, or not.
— Deuteronomy 8:2-3

When a person goes through the agony of a marriage ending, it is far too easy to fall into sin or aggravated temptation to sin. Issues of gossip, judgment (whether justified or not), adultery, extreme anger, and temptation to despair can arise.

This chapter is not included to add insult to injury, but rather to address the fact that *sin steals our joy*. If we intend to find joy following a divorce, we must have an honest conversation about what can pull us away from that joy.

There is an old Alcoholics Anonymous rule that says that we fall into bad patterns when we are "hungry, sick, angry, lonely, or tired." Let's face it: divorce can bring about at least three of those five elements.

When angry we are open to fall into temptations of gossiping about our ex-spouse, criticizing others, or even lying or exaggerating another's part in our pain. Similarly, we may not be completely honest about our own shortcomings, and, in an effort to seek support, we paint ourselves as the victim who bears no responsibility for the breakup of the union. I fell into this pattern myself.

An example of anger coming out sideways is in the parent who constantly talks about his own feelings of anger and hurt in front of his children. Frustration, fear, and infuriation slip into every conversation, often within earshot of his children. The children are in the middle of a battle, having to choose sides and alliances. As this man suffers his own pain, he can become blind to the additional pain he brings onto his children.

Pope Francis, in one of his weekly audiences, stated his opposition to this behavior like this, saying, "Never, never, never take the child as a hostage!" He warned against allowing children to be "used" as a way to hurt or get back at each other or as bargaining chips in negotiations. He cautioned, "Frequently the child is taken hostage and the father speaks ill of the mother, and the mother speaks ill of the father, and so much harm is done."[1] In *Amoris Laetitia*, Pope Francis states, "The divorced and remarried should ask themselves: how did they act towards their children when the conjugal union entered into crisis[?]" (300).

When tired, we give in to temptations more easily. We become vulnerable to acting out on the anger or loneliness we are feeling. This inhibits us from finding positive solutions or can tempt us to give in to behaviors that are undesirable because we lack the energy to fight them.

In an effort to dull the intense pain felt when a relationship falls apart, substance abuse or addiction concerns may arise. Seeking help for problems such as these are a vital component to reclaiming joy.

Another vital component in our reclamation of joy is found in the sacraments. We can sustain ourselves through the sacraments. Reconciliation and the Eucharist, in particular, can strengthen us during these struggles.

Prayer

Dear heavenly Father, when I am hurt it is so easy to want to strike back. Please help me to measure my words and actions with prayer. Help me to seek the Sacrament of Reconciliation if needed.

Questions for Reflection

1. Has pain led me into sinful places?

2. Do I need to seek reconciliation with anyone and/or with God?

3. When have I last examined my conscience and gone to confession?

4. Have I used my children as a pawn in my divorce or failed to protect them from additional harm in my own actions?

CHAPTER THREE

Should I Stay or Should I Go Now

"Will you also go away?"
— John 6:67

"First my husband left me, and then the Church said our marriage wasn't real! He was able to marry the woman he cheated on me with, and the Church approved it. That is why I stopped going to the Catholic Church!" — T

"The Church wanted money for me to get an annulment. They are just trying to make money off my pain so I can get a 'Catholic divorce'!" — D

"I thought it took two people to get married and two people should decide if there would be a divorce. How can the Church grant an annulment if I never wanted my marriage to end?" — B

These are real thoughts conveyed to me by people who decided to leave the Church following their divorces. While it may be convenient to imply they may not have had a clear understanding of the sacramentality of the state of matrimony and the annulment process, their pain is very real and we, as Christians, need to acknowledge and address these concerns.

I also met people who did not think the Church should judge their marriage or the circumstances of its demise. They left the Catholic Church to remarry in a Christian tradition, but outside the "rules and procedures" the Catholic Church would require. They still wanted to worship God but did not want to apply for an annulment or wait the needed time period to be free to remarry in the Catholic Church. In my interviews, I was often given the "We are all sinners; why should my sin be considered worse than anyone else's?" response.

These people had a desire for faith but did not want to deal with what they interpreted as "rules." Instead of embracing the Church's wisdom in expecting permanence for marriage and the healing process of annulment, they felt injured by it.

The third group of people who struggled with the Church's teachings and whether or not to leave the Church were those who remarried outside the Church but subsequently applied for an annulment and had the new union blessed by the Church. Couples who chose this path usually loved the Eucharist and truly desired to live within the Church's teachings but felt an urgency to remarry and were inhibited by the length of time the annulment process took. It is clear that to find joy following the end of a marriage we must first understand the things that pull us away from the Church, which in itself contains a path to joy.

———

God created shadows to better emphasize the light.
— Pope St. John XXIII

———

Prayer
God, it is truly hard to understand the way things are done through your Catholic Church sometimes. Please heal any hurts that individuals inside your Church may have caused me and help me to humbly consider the healing process of annulment.

Questions for Reflection

1. Am I considering leaving (or have I left) the Catholic Church because my point of view was challenged by its catechism?

2. Have I tried to make over God's law in my own image rather than see the wisdom of Christ's instruction in his Church?

3. Am I suffering from extreme hurt as a result of how I think the Church has handled my divorce? Should I seek spiritual counseling about this issue?

CHAPTER FOUR

The Waiting Is the Hardest Part (the Challenges of Getting an Annulment)

*I consider that the sufferings of this present time
are not worth comparing with the glory
that is to be revealed to us.*
— Romans 8:18

I hit a wall of complaints and concerns about the annulment process. In the past, some dioceses charged a fee for the paperwork to be processed, and the cost was quite prohibitive. How a parish or diocese handles this challenge can be the difference between someone deciding to stay in the Catholic Church or to leave.

Because of this, Pope Francis has encouraged dioceses to abandon the fee completely. In past circumstances, an individual's parish may have picked up the cost for the annulment process. One woman told me a parish priest gave her the money for her annulment and told her to "pay it forward" one day and help someone in a similar position.

Some petitioners perceive this practice of charging fees as unfair to them because they are trying to do things the way the Church instructs, but that means that they may not able to pursue an annulment for financial reasons. If you have found yourself to be in this position, I would urge you to look into the annulment process now as things have changed so dramatically.

Timing is everything. I met my (now) husband before my annulment had been granted and his had not yet begun. I had been having fertility issues in my previous marriage (which led to some of our problems) and was advised by doctors that I had a very small window of opportunity to pursue pregnancy. As a result, my husband and I felt we should marry as soon as possible to increase the possibility of having children. (Disclaimer: If I knew then about the Catholic faith what I know now, I would have trusted God to deal with the fertility issues.) If we had fully understood the Church's teachings and reasoning on this subject, I believe we would have waited. We were married by a nondenominational Christian minister. It took about two years to have our annulments granted, and we were pregnant with our third child by then. We immediately went to confession and had our marriage blessed by the Catholic Church. This situation still brings me some pain when I consider it today.

I recognize that the length of the annulment process can push some away from marrying in the Church. When we are seeking joy, this issue and the perfection in the patience of waiting need to be emphasized. The problems with pursuing an annulment are obvious, but what may not be as obvious are the healing process and blessings that it brings.

The process begins by meeting with a priest to review what the tribunal will need. You typically must provide your marriage certificate, divorce papers, and a statement of review of you and your spouse's time together (including courtship). Finally, the tribunal reaches out to those who had knowledge of your relationship and asks for a statement/questionnaire from them about what they witnessed during the duration of that time. (This is not typically shared with you.)

The annulment process (for us) was lengthy and detailed, but I was able to conduct an autopsy of sorts on my time with my ex-spouse as a result of this difficult process. I recognized my own immaturity at the time of our union, the patterns I had developed that were destructive and prohibitive of growth, and the misunderstandings I had about marriage at the time we were joined. It was an eye-opening experience. I found healing in the sense that I had blamed my ex-husband for all the pain during our breakup. While he had made some terrible choices, I could now see what led me into that relationship and some of the responsibility I shared in its demise. From this insight, I was able to go on to have a much healthier union the second time. The things I discovered also helped me let go of some of the anger I had felt toward my former spouse. There is also a sense of peace in knowing my former union was not truly a valid union and my current state of matrimony is.

In a desire for more information on the subject of this booklet, I sought the advice of a deacon I know who serves on our local tribunal, Deacon James P. Steiger, case instructor for the Diocese of Rochester, New York. "The best advice to give people is that they should begin the annulment process as soon as their divorce is final if they think they have grounds for an annulment," he said. "They should not wait until they are in another relationship and considering marriage."

The "waiting" can be made a little easier by doing a few things:

1. *Fully understand the annulment process and how long it takes.* Most priests, tribunal members, and divorced/annulled people I spoke with agree that the average time it takes for an annulment to be granted has been about a year. This is not a fixed time limit; my husband's took two years. Currently, due to the changes in the process that were led by Pope Francis, an annulment may be granted in six to nine months! You can discuss the process at length with your local priest, and the tribunal generally provides you with a list of steps in the process.

2. *Fill the time with positive growth.* Consider using this time to deepen your own faith journey through retreats, readings, classes, Bible studies, or other spiritual endeavors. If we are engaging in activity, the time does not drag along. If you have had emotional damage from your marriage or its demise, consider spending this time in counseling. If we design this time to be a healing time, we can emerge from this experience stronger emotionally and spiritually.

3. *Remember: receiving an annulment is not guaranteed.* A knowledgeable priest should be able to guide you in whether you might have grounds to proceed, but the tribunal will ultimately make the decision.

———

We always find that those who walked closest to Christ were those who had to bear the greatest trials.
— St. Teresa of Ávila

———

Prayer
Dear Lord, please give me the courage to be honest with myself and the tribunal as I move forth in the annulment process. Give me the patience I need to wait for the results and the inspiration to grow in faith during that time.

Questions for Reflection

1. Have I been afraid to pursue an annulment?
   If so, why? Because of judgment, fear of hurt,
   or fear it will not be granted?

2. Have I considered that the annulment process may heal me?

3. Have I made an appointment to speak to my
   priest about the annulment process?

4. If I have received an annulment, did it reveal
   to me areas I need to work on in myself, and
   have I thanked God for that wisdom?

CHAPTER FIVE

Finding Joy in Following Christ

On waking, I shall be content in your presence.
Lord, when your glory appears, my joy will be full.
— Psalm 17:15 (from the Lectionary)

As I conducted interview after interview for this book, I was encouraged to discover a constant among those Catholics who continued to practice their faith under the most trying of circumstances. This commonality was a true understanding of the Church's teachings on the Eucharist and a reverence for Christ in the Blessed Sacrament.

A Personal Eucharist Story

I remarried outside of the Catholic Church and found myself as a devout, daily-Mass-going Catholic in an irregular marriage. My husband and I worked from day one to obtain annulments and move toward convalidating (what we felt in our hearts was) a valid union.

Our dear priest wanted to support us in every
pastoral way possible, and he was my weekly
confessor. However, in his desire to be pastoral, he never informed me that I should not
be receiving the Eucharist. Maybe he thought
I knew and was choosing to ignore the teaching; in reality, I didn't understand the obligation to receive the sacrament in a state of
grace. Living outside of God's plan for my
marriage put me outside of that grace.

Years later (after my marriage had been
blessed), I grew in my comprehension of
these issues. In my priest's attempt to be pastoral, I suffered grief and guilt over my mis-
take. I have since confessed all of this and rec-
onciled my situation, but I still wince when I
think back on my error to this day.

I met one couple, Paul and Beth, who had
remarried without the benefit of annulments or
the blessings of the Church. However, the Eucharist was so important to them that after going to
confession and discussing the situation with their
priest, they chose to live platonically until their annulments were granted so they could once again
receive the Eucharist.

Fred and Mary, in an almost identical situation, chose to refrain from receiving the Eucharist
(as instructed by the Church) until they had their

previous marriages annulled and their current legal marriage blessed (convalidated) as a sacrament by the Catholic Church. They attended Mass daily, and the desire and longing to receive Jesus in the Blessed Sacrament was palpable. I witnessed it daily on their faces and longed to share in the joy of communion with them one day. It was a beautiful reminder to pray for our separated brothers and sisters in Christ.

Lauren chose to stay chaste and not have a relationship following her divorce out of a strong love for Christ and a desire to receive him in the Eucharist. Her desire for Christ outweighed her physical longing for male companionship. She has had her marriage annulled and, should she meet the right person, is open to the idea of having a sacramental marriage. Until that day, she vows chastity.

Still more un-remarried Catholics didn't realize that following a civil divorce they could (after a good confession) receive the Eucharist as long as they were not in a (physical) relationship with a member of the opposite sex. Julie, upon hearing this, cried tears of joy as she expressed how she had stayed away from Jesus for so long and how painful it had been.

One of my favorite stories, however, came from a woman who had remarried. Since she had not pursued an annulment, Carol remarried civilly outside the Church. Eventually, her husband became Catholic and they had their previous marriages annulled by the Church. She had refrained (rightly) from receiving the Eucharist during this time, so on the day her marriage was blessed, she and her husband received the Eucharist together. She told me it was a "virginal" experience for her — to be joined in the sacrament of holy matrimony with her spouse and joined in true communion with Jesus in the Eucharist.

Carol also shared that she found a stronger faith in going through this entire process. She had drifted earlier in her life, but Christ used this pain and the sweet anticipation of waiting to be joined with him in the Eucharist to create a much stronger bond with God than she had experienced before.

Love of Christ in the Eucharist and remaining Catholic following a divorce are intrinsically linked. Perhaps when seeking joy, we should start with the source and summit of joy! We will find this in the Catholic Church's teaching on the Eucharist based on John 6:19-67: that the bread and wine become the true body, blood, soul, and divinity of Christ. There are special considerations when in an "irregular relationship." Though Church teaching is clear on these matters, Pope Francis encourages faithful Catholics to talk with their parish priest about their situation.

———

Joy is a net of love by which we catch souls.
— (Mother) St. Teresa of Calcutta

———

Prayer

Lord, reveal yourself to me in the Eucharist! Help me to see you — body, blood, soul, and divinity.

Questions for Reflection

1. Have I been taught the reality of Christ's presence in the Eucharist?

2. If I am considering leaving the Church, have I thought about the reality of walking away from Jesus in the sacraments?

3. Have I sought the advice of a priest in regards to receiving the Eucharist in my particular state of life and situation?

CHAPTER SIX

How Is the Church Trying to Help? Your Church Walks with You

When the Spirit of truth comes, he will guide you into all the truth ... he will declare to you the things that are to come.
— John 16:13

The Church has always been aware and sensitive to the pain of her members. This is made abundantly clear in this quote from Pope St. John Paul II:

> However, let these men and women know that the Church loves them, that she is not far from them and suffers because of their situation. The divorced and remarried are and remain her members, because they have received baptism and retain their Christian faith.[2]

In his address in 1997 to the thirteenth plenary assembly of the Pontifical Council for the Family, St. John Paul II focused on three areas of need regarding divorced Catholics: instruction regarding fidelity, support of families in difficulty, and spiritual guidance. Following the assembly, the council issued recommendations for "Care of the Divorced and Remarried," stating:

> In many countries, divorce has become a true social "plague" (cf. *Guadium et Spes*, 47).... The Church is extremely sensitive to the sorrow of her members: just as she rejoices with those who rejoice, she weeps with those who weep (cf. Rom 12:15).[3]

Pope Francis attributed the marriage crisis to people who "don't know the sacrament, the beauty of the sacrament." He also said, "They do not know what indissoluble means, they do not know that it is for a lifetime. It is difficult" (Address at the Opening of the Pastoral Congress of the Diocese of Rome, June 16, 2016).

Clearly, the Church is aware of the modern times and the conflict between teachings on marriage and the way individuals are actually conducting themselves. As with most conflict, pain and distress are usually the result of this type of disconnect.

I have outlined the three common concerns I have heard from divorced Catholics regarding the Catholic Church and divorce: the perceived or actual injury caused by the members of the Church in response to a couple's divorce, the difficulty and the perceived cost of annulments, and the desire for the Sacraments of Eucharist and Penance.

Pope Francis convened the 2014-15 synod on marriage and family so the Church could look at the very issues discussed above.

———

In the Extraordinary Synod, the procedures, the processes were discussed, and there is a concern for streamlining the procedures for reasons of justice. Justice, so they may be just, and justice for the people who are waiting.... Some procedures are so long or so onerous that they do not facilitate them, and the people leave.... And Mother Church must do justice and say: "Yes, it's true, your marriage is annulled — No, your marriage is valid." But justice has to say it. This way they can move forward without this doubt, this darkness in their spirit.[4]
— Pope Francis

———

The Pope reminds us to be pastoral in the care of those divorced Catholics: "The logic of integration is the key to their pastoral care, a care which would allow them not only to realize that they belong to the Church as the body of Christ, but also to know that they can have a joyful and fruitful experience in it" (*Amoris Laetitia*, 299). *Relatio Synodi*, a summary document of the 2014 synod, confirms this, stating, "All families should, above all, be treated with respect and love and accompanied on their journey as Christ accompanied the disciples on the road to Emmaus" (46).

The public often expresses concern that the Church is removed from understanding the struggles of "regular people." I would assert that this synod, the conferences, and ongoing discussions prove the opposite. The Church has a special window into the suffering of humans in all their conditions. I believe that, led by the Holy Spirit, the Church will continue to find the best path to assist us in all our needs while helping us to grow in faith and understanding along the way.

———

Christ said, "I am the Truth"; he did not say,
"I am the custom."
— St. Toribio

———

Prayer

Dearest Lord, you promised that our Church would be led by the Holy Spirit. Please be with our Church now as she struggles to best help your people.

Questions for Reflection

1. Do I believe, in my heart, that the Catholic Church is led by the Holy Spirit?

2. Can I be humble enough to follow the instruction of the Church on these matters?

3. Do I believe that the Church has true compassion for its divorced members?

Conclusion

Other Ways to Find Joy

O Lord my God, I cried to you for help,
and you have healed me.
— Psalm 30:2

In conclusion, the three things that can be burdensome in going through a divorce — the emotional hurt, annulment process, and separation from the sacraments — can ultimately be the cause of much joy. In educating and challenging ourselves on the Church's teachings and reasoning behind those teachings, and in how the Church offers help in dealing with each of those areas, we can grow in faith, love, and understanding. Both Pope Francis and St. John Paul II emphasize a call to "graduality." This means that the Church reaches out to those in pain, less in judgment and more with mercy. The focus is on meeting individuals where they are but not leaving them there. The goal changes (through mercy and love) from reacting with rules to informing consciences with love. An attitude from the suffering person of humility and love for the Church is "essential for avoiding the grave danger of misunderstandings, such as the notion that any priest can quickly grant 'exceptions' or that some people can obtain sacramental privileges in exchange for favors" (*Amoris Laetitia*, 300).

———

Conversation with the priest, in the internal forum, contributes to the formation of a correct judgment on what hinders the possibility of a fuller participation in the life of the Church and on what steps can foster it and make it grow.
— Amoris Laetitia, *300*

———

There are many ways to reclaim joy during the process of recovery from a divorce. The biggest key to discovering hope is to remain in God's grace through his Church and the sacraments.

Confession is so very healing! Receiving this sacrament can provide a chance to look at patterns of sin, to see our mistakes, and to get some good spiritual guidance. This sacrament provides sanctifying grace (brings you back to God and reminds you of his love) and actual grace (strengthens you against future sinfulness by giving you the grace to resist some temptations). If reconciliation alone is not enough, consider finding a spiritual director to help you get through this experience.

Many churches now offer support groups for separated or divorced Catholics. These groups can help overcome some of the loneliness and feelings of isolation that divorce and separation often bring. Having a safe place to share struggles, and even joys and successes, can provide a healthy outlet.

Allowing others to know that we need help in parenting issues, with economic concerns, and in dealing with loneliness — and even that we are in need of practical advice — will help us grow in humility, faithfulness, and joy. When we allow others in and give them the opportunity to assist us in our need, we are creating an avenue for grace for them as well.

When struggling with any issue we can look to the example of the saints to inspire and instruct us. St. Helena (mother of Constantine and the one who is said to have discovered the true cross of Jesus) is one such saint. Her husband is reported to have left her to marry another woman who would help advance his career status. It must have been heartbreaking for Helena, but she continued through her life with grace and virtue.

We should also study and pray sacred Scripture. Contemplating the inspired word provides guidance and, often, inspiration in difficult circumstances. Happiness is fleeting, but joy in the Lord will sustain us no matter how difficult our obstacles seem to be.

If you are seeking companionship, tell friends that you are ready to open your heart to possibilities again and join clubs or committees at church to expand the pool of potential friendships or relationships in your future.

Finally, remember the power of prayer. Consider joining a prayer group or Bible study, or attending a retreat or Cursillo. When we are filling our time with love and knowledge of the Lord, we remember that "with God all things are possible" (Mt 19:26).

RESOURCES AND SOURCES

Amoris Laetitia, Pope Francis (Our Sunday Visitor, 2016). Also available at: w2.vatican.va/content/ francesco/en/apost_exhortations.index.html

Excerpts from the *Lectionary for Mass for Use in the Dioceses of the United States of America, second typical edition* © 2001, 1998, 1997, 1986, 1970 Confraternity of Christian Doctrine, Inc., Washington, DC. Used with permission. All rights reserved. No portion of this text may be reproduced by any means without permission in writing from the copyright owner.

Quotations from papal and other Vatican-generated documents available on vatican.va are copyright © Libreria Editrice Vaticana.

The Pastoral Care of the Divorced and Remarried, Pontifical Council for the Family (Pauline Books and Media, 1997).

Relatio Synodi, "The Pastoral Challenges of the Family in Context of Evangelization." The III Extraordinary General Assembly of the Synod of Bishops, October 2014.

Interviews

Interviews were conducted with Deacon James P. Steiger, Case Instructor, Roman Catholic Diocese of Rochester Tribunal, and with divorced Catholics who wish to remain anonymous.

References

[1] General Audience, May 20, 2015. https://w2vatican.va/content/francesco/en/audiences/2015/documents/papa-francesco_20150520_udienza-generale.html

[2] Address of His Holiness Pope John Paul II to the Pontifical Council for the Family, January 24, 1997. https://w2.vatican.va/content/john-paul-ii/en/speeches/1997/january/documents/hf_jp-ii_spe_19970124_pont-cons-family.html

[3] Recommendation for the Care of "Divorced," Pontifical Council for the Family (originally published in *L'Osservatore Romano*, Weekly Edition in English, March 6, 1997). https://www.ewtn.com/library/CURIA/PCFDIVOR.HTM

[4] Greetings of His Holiness Pope Francis to Participants in a Course on Marriage Organized by the Tribunal of the Roman Rota, November 5, 2014. https://w2.vatican.va/content/francesco/en/speeches/2014/november/documents/papa-francesco_20141105_tribunale-rota-romana.html